GW00758863

Encounters with mental distress: Quaker stories

First published in May 2015

Quaker Books, Friends House, 173 Euston Road, London NW1 2BJ

www.quaker.org.uk

Developed by the Mental Health in Meetings Cluster of the Quaker Life Network

© Britain Yearly Meeting of the Religious Society of Friends (Quakers) 2015
Registered charity number 1127633

ISBN 978 1 907123 86 3
eISBN 978 1 907123 87 0

Designed and typeset by Gabrielle Scott

Printed by CM Print Ltd, Brighton

Contents

Foreword

This book came about as a result of a number of strands within Britain Yearly Meeting coming together, leading to a meeting in York in October 2011. Following this, Quaker Life agreed to support the work of a Mental Health Cluster Core Group.

It was apparent that both individuals and meetings were having difficulties in being with mental health problems, so we asked for stories which Friends were willing to share in this book.

As Quakers, we believe that there is "that of God" in everyone, no matter what. This is fundamental to us and therefore something that we need to incorporate into our meeting's life without question. Friends can find it very hard to live up to this when they are attempting to be with someone with a mental health problem – perhaps also being uncertain of their own emotional response to the issues and not knowing what to do get in the way. This book aims to reduce the fear that is often felt when people are faced with mental illness or distress by offering personal insights. We hope that it will increase understanding, reduce stigma and enable people to be more open, more compassionate and more accepting of those who are distressed or ill.

It is important to us to foster truth in our meetings and to "seek to know one another in the things which are eternal". Friends with mental health problems may be very wary of being open about them because misunderstanding and prejudice still exist, even among Friends. Also, meetings may be reluctant to address any difficulties or conflicts which arise for all sorts of reasons. Conflict and the fear of openness on the part of individuals or meetings as a whole may lead to Friends leaving meetings and to stop going to any Quaker meeting. Are we able and willing to hear about someone else's reality, even when it is strange and disturbing to us?

> "I have found that it is only when I act, trusting in the urgings of the Spirit, even though I may not understand why I am doing it, that I feel free from fear. This is what I call acting with love."
>
> *Peter Allen-Williams*
> *Towards a Quaker View of Mental Health Conference, March 2014*

We offer this book in the hope that it will be read with open minds, enabling Friends to understand more and therefore to act with greater love.

Isobel Lane

Acknowledgements

This book has been a project of the Mental Health in Meetings Cluster of the Quaker Life Network. It has been overseen by the Core Group of that cluster who have been responsible for seeing the project through. The group comprises Isobel Lane, Jane Muers, Peter Allen-Williams and Stephan Ball, and support has been given by Oliver Waterhouse as Quaker Life staff member responsible for this area of work. Thanks go to all of them for their work.

The Core Group would like to thank for their contribution to the editing of this book Barbara Mitchells and Jez Smith. They have both given huge amounts of their time and experience in proofreading and copy-editing. And for helping to get the text of the stories into a format that shares the stories in the way that we think is most powerful for the reader.

We are grateful to the Britain Yearly Meeting Publications Team for their work in getting the book ready for publication.

Our greatest thanks go to the people who have been willing to share their stories with us and made this publication possible.

Introduction

Issues relating to mental illness and mental distress have been of particular interest and concern to Quakers at various times during the history of the Religious Society of Friends. In 1796 a concern of early Friends led to the setting up of The Retreat psychiatric hospital in York. Some of the more recent involvements include: a Young Friends concern and appeal for mental health in the early 2000s; Mental Health in our Meetings courses for elders and overseers; special interest groups at Yearly Meetings; the Retreat lecture; and the setting up of the Quaker Life Network Cluster on Mental Health.

It was in response to Isobel Lane's article in *The Friend* on 24 May 2013 that Quakers started to share stories of their experience of mental illness. The request was broad because at that time we had not decided what to do with them. It was a leading, and with the same faith that guides Quakers in many decisions, we followed it.

Stories started to come in. It took a while before the Mental Health Core Group decided what to do with them. Initially, we were hoping to discover from Friends what their experience has been, what sort of things were happening in meetings and how those meetings were coping. We knew that there would be a huge diversity in what was happening and we also knew that there would be a great variation in the way that meetings responded to different situations.

The Core Group has also had its own story about the way that the stories have come into print. We asked for people to share their experiences and asked all the contributors to let us know if they would be happy to have that story shared in its entirety or whether they would prefer it to be anonymised to protect them. On reading through the stories and starting work on the book, anonymity was a topic that was regularly being discussed. Looking at the themes that came up in many of the stories, we felt that it was not only the people who have shared their stories, but also others around them that may need to be protected. It took some time before we finally decided that it would be best for all of the stories to be completely anonymous to try to protect any person or meeting that we felt might be easily identifiable. It wasn't until we first started working on a draft that we discovered that anonymising the stories was going to be a big piece of work. The first draft broke up the stories and clustered them with others that had similar themes. On reflection it didn't feel right for the group to be directing Friends to read the stories in a particular way or to impose our interpretation onto the text.

On most occasions we have been able to keep the stories in their entirety. However, we have removed identifying information and in a few cases we felt it necessary to shorten them; and this is what is presented here. Now we have a series of stories that share open and honest accounts of a range of issues present in meetings and the essential power of the stories remains. On the whole through editing we inevitably lose some of the spiritual and emotional impact that comes from the very personal nature of many of the stories, yet the power of those stories remains. We hope it now feels more readable and accessible to the reader, whether Quaker or not.

The result is a collection of stories. As with the confidentiality issue, it was not a straightforward process deciding how to present the material. While thought has gone into the order and in some cases themes do appear to be close together, this was not the deciding factor. Much of the order is simply down to how the stories read together and support one another.

You will find the occasional name printed in the stories. We have not assumed that these have been changed by the author and so have changed them all to be doubly sure that they are not identifiable. We are also aware that some people may think that they recognise events from some of the stories and so may think that they can identify the author and the circumstances. This may be the case, but there is a word of caution in this and it is one that I have learned from other aspects of my work. It is that while the area of mental health is very diverse, many similar mental health experiences, behaviours and life situations are played out in more than one place. In reading this, you may think that you recognise a story, but it may just be that it is a situation that is taking place somewhere else as well as in a meeting that is known to you.

After reflection we have decided not to include a section on defining the illnesses and conditions that are identified in this book as there are many different ways to view mental distress and illness. Instead we have highlighted the main websites offering resources including background information and leaflets. If what you are looking for is not listed there then a web-search of the particular issue or problem offers many results.

We want the stories to stand on their own and we are immensely grateful to all those who have sent in their stories and to everyone who has shared a story informally. If any of these stories are meaningful to you in any way we hope that reading this book will help you, and all those who are involved with mental health issues in meetings, towards greater communication, mutual understanding and compassionate care. If it does this, then it has fulfilled its purpose.

Oliver Waterhouse

A copy of Isobel Lane's article, published in *The Friend* on 24 May 2013, is available to read at the end of this book.

Quaker stories

Things like this are much less 'scary' if one can talk about them!

It is important to us 'mental' Friends (horrid word!) to be accepted and supported by our local meetings. We don't bite! It may take a little courage, but all that is needed is a friendly enquiry about our general 'health', much as one would enquire about someone's recent operation or troublesome cough. A little sincere appreciation of some unusual ministry helps self-confidence considerably – treat the patient as a 'normal' person (as indeed we are), and be solicitous without being condescending. I once related what I considered to be a very valuable 'hallucination' that I had experienced, and only then realised that I had given away the fact of my state of mental health. No one said anything.

If you're feeling brave, invite people to tea! I remember being very much cheered by some excellent scones made by an elderly and sympathetic Friend. I don't remember any words of wisdom but I always went home with my depression considerably lightened.

At the moment I'm trying to come to terms with a terminal prognosis. I'm not at all bothered by the news – I'm 80 and have had a very full life, but it really upsets me that Friends in my local meeting won't (or can't) talk to me about death, or even let me talk to them about it. Perhaps I'm being unreasonable, but I did expect some support from local Quakers. Things like this are much less 'scary' if one can talk about them!

I continue to have mild depression but...

I first came to a Quaker meeting some 15 years ago and immediately felt at home. It was a big meeting but was always a good place to come to. I didn't shout out or do anything that obvious but was always accepted when I was feeling low and was occasionally tearful. That was important. More recently I was in a small meeting during a period when I was being bullied at work. My need then was more obvious and Friends there were very supportive.

I've also been able to give support to Friends and others when they were mentally distressed. This kind of support, given and received, is part of being a community, being human.

Over the years I've been prescribed various medications, which I took for periods but I've never felt that this was a solution. I had to find the underlying cause. I'm aware that very many people suffer mental illness to a greater or lesser degree. Why is this?

In my case I think it's due to the moral expectations and contradictions I was raised with. I was expected: to be moral; to get qualifications and have a career; be polite and obedient; to put others first; to look down on certain sections of society; to live within my means and not to plead poverty; to stop war and save the whale. These were in a framework of mechanistic materialism, social Darwinism. I'd only feel successful in my family if I could meet these expectations. In wider society success is measured by conspicuous consumption, which is counter to my values.

At meeting I could simply be me. The wisdom of Quaker writings corresponded with how I was, but was marred by some Friends' frantic busyness.

I now feel that I've turned a corner. I'm working creatively, nurturing my spiritual development and pursuing, at a gentle pace, my own concern for social justice. My experience of having depression and being bullied are important parts of my journey so far. I continue to have mild depression but I feel able to accept it as part of me and cope, without tumbling into a pit of despair.

I was diagnosed as having bipolar disorder

My experiences of being a Quaker with a mental illness have been mixed, some profoundly moving and vital, and some distressing. I have included descriptions of both.

I attended a city meeting (not the one of my membership) for several years. I felt that I belonged; I made friends, joined social activities connected to the meeting, and valued the spirit I felt in meetings. Several of the people I met during that time have become close friends. I was fairly involved in the life of the meeting although I was shy to offer to take roles (such as committees or starting groups) in the meeting like others had done. Eventually I was asked to take on a position, about which I was really pleased and thought I could make a strong contribution. On several occasions I was on the point of asking to transfer my membership.

On one occasion, I was asked to run a workshop for the meeting's weekend away. I was pleased to be asked, and felt keen to prove I could contribute, but had, during the past six months, become more and more unwell and depressed, until I was on the brink of suicide. Four hours before I was due to arrive at the weekend away, I telephoned to explain that I had collapsed and been referred to the emergency mental health team. That weekend was a dark and terrifying time for me, but I soon received a card, with a beautiful painting on it, signed by everyone at the weekend away to say that they wished me well and missed me.

If you are sick and frightened and alone, if God seems far away from you, as your body and your mind are fragile and fractured, you may think that a gesture like sending a card would barely register, but I can tell you that's not true. That card meant the world to me. At that time, I thought that no one could appreciate where I was. I still believed the depression was my fault, that I was defective, or not trying hard enough to fight through the fog of despair that had come down on me, so to get a card from my meeting, my spiritual home that acknowledged that there was an understanding – it was significant. The card stayed on my mantelpiece for months afterwards, all through that dark time, it was there as a reminder that I had a place somewhere, and that I was being held in the light.

But another experience was painful and hurtful and has resulted in me not attending any meeting since that time, although I still proudly identify myself as a Quaker. It is something fundamental to my being, and because of this, my experience probably cuts more deeply. What happened was certainly not down to malice, nor indifference. A large part of it is the fault of mental illness itself. Unfortunately being in mental distress doesn't lend itself well to active participation. It is really easy to become invisible to the world, because you are not able to take part in it. So, despite my feelings of hurt – and they are 'my' feelings, tangled up in all sorts of things to do with 'me' – there is no blame intended in this. I do think however that some of the ways Quaker meetings, particularly the larger ones, handle things, may be unwittingly discriminating against those with mental distress.

After my first breakdown I had a period of recovery followed by a period of working very hard, with long hours. So I didn't attend meeting a lot. No one contacted me, which I didn't think much of, but it was quite frustrating that the few times I did attend people whom I knew quite well (such as elders, overseers or other regular attenders) would come up and ask me if it was the first time I'd been to the meeting or a Quaker meeting at all.

Then I had another breakdown, which lasted for seventeen months. I did go to meeting a few times during this period. I was afraid to go a lot of the time. I felt that the crushing feeling of darkness inside me would be so overwhelming that I knew I had been deserted. But I did go sometimes. I found it really hard. The illness had decimated my confidence and I was paralysed by social anxiety. The dread of the meeting finishing and me sitting on my own, no one talking to me, of coming out for tea and standing awkwardly as cheerful faces and people around me seemed so at ease settled on me and often meant I fled as soon as notices were over. Because of the meeting's size and location it often had new people experiencing the silence for the first time. Sometimes someone would minister about what a profound experience it was. Sometimes people would minister about their suffering and how they felt held. I watched as members of the meeting would flock to welcome that new person or offer support and condolence to them. I sat alone and I felt only sorrow. It felt like a place where bleakness and anger and the ugliness of mental illness didn't really have a place. And I wanted to have a place there so much.

I was functioning on some level during parts of this, and one of the things I did continue to do was attend to my responsibilities for the position I was offered in the life of the meeting, albeit sporadically. My co-convener was lovely and supportive and helpful, but others in the meeting rarely talked to me, or knew my name. In the end I confided in her that I couldn't come for a while because I was unwell. She was utterly compassionate in her response.

I didn't attend for almost a year and as a result I was un-nominated, in my absence, without anyone contacting me. I was really hurt. It wasn't so much that I had been passed over, more that the meeting seemed to have been completely unaware that I had been absent. I know people *did* know a little because my friends who went to the meeting said that people often asked after me. But no one ever got in touch to wonder why I hadn't been seen at the meeting for a long time.

I wrote – in some anger I confess – to explain that I felt discriminated against. I asked my email to be referred to elders so I could raise the matter. I was just hoping that someone would read about my suffering and reach out to me, to welcome me back and say I still had a place in that spiritual home. But the individual to whom I wrote did not pass my email on, and only wrote back in very brusque terms to ask if I'd decided whether I wanted to be nominated or not because the committee were meeting soon, and they needed to know.

At that point I copied in elders I knew (who had responded so kindly the first time) and I did receive an immediate compassionate response from both of them, for which I was deeply grateful, but by that time it felt too late to go back. Because I suffer social anxiety and am prone to bouts of depression triggered by this, although I have had good intentions, I haven't been able to go to a Quaker meeting since.

However, I still feel held in some respects. Although I haven't been there for years, the meeting where my membership remains have overwhelmed me with their kindness. I have received cards, scripture and messages by people I don't know well as well as those I do. I have been held in the light and been regularly included on 'the list' in healing meetings. I am glad because it means I still feel I have a good connection to Friends. It is my faith and it is my leading. I am a Quaker and I always will be.

I write this because in every meeting there are probably those who are suffering in silence. Stigma is still extreme if you have a mental illness, so it's not easy to bring up unless you feel totally comfortable. A Quaker meeting can be a place to heal, but if there is not an acknowledgement that there is terrible darkness and fear and sometimes the light does not seem to penetrate, then it can seem like it is only a place for you if you are happy and open and can share. I had a lot of people to help me. Individual friends (who are also Friends) offered me solace and kindness. But what went wrong for me was that the meeting itself seemed unaware and uninterested in me. I was suffering and no one knew it, because no one had noticed I was gone.

They trusted in me...

I had a major breakdown while on a psychiatric social work course when I was 23 – before I became a Quaker. My employers were not always sympathetic. I am bipolar. I can cope with the depressive elements, but need short hospital admissions when I go high. I have had excellent psychotherapy and my condition, with the help of medication, has remained stable for more than 20 years. The acceptance of Friends has been important and has meant a lot to me. They trusted in me, even when I had difficulty in trusting myself.

We don't think we could have acted sooner

We had a man arrive from another place. He was plausible, pleasant and easy.

He was put up in the flat of a Friend in the meeting and for some weeks all was well. The man became more difficult and unpredictable. He caused great problems. Eventually he stormed out of meeting shouting and being extremely rude.

The Friend then had to call the police and have him evicted from the flat. The police said we should have alerted them to the problems as they cannot react to the first call. They would have come as soon as we asked on the Sunday if they had known the difficulties.

We eventually discovered that he had stopped taking his medication.

He said he was going back to his wife. We understand he had caused problems at another meeting and was asked to leave.

We alerted our area meeting to him.

We are not sure we could have been wiser any sooner!

I was asking far too much of myself, too soon

I realise now that I was asking far too much of myself, too soon.

Statistically, 'mental illness' is so widespread that it is certain that many in our meetings will have been affected at one time or another, and may be 'suffering in silence'.

Some years ago, I was a member of a meeting. My husband used to say that he couldn't possibly sit still for an hour, and would much rather be doing an hour's gardening or 'something useful'! He became ill and died. After his death I plunged into a deep depression, coupled with anxiety, on top of the grief. My GP referred me to the psychiatrist, and I was greatly helped by therapy and medication.

During this period I returned to meeting. Friends were sympathetic to my loss, of course, but as the months passed, the meeting continued 'as normal', but for me things never reverted to 'normal'. I found that the silence, in particular, was unbearable at this time. Silence, in fact, was associated in my mind with a deep existential fear and dread, which exhibited itself as a permanent 'silent scream' inside my head, which made it impossible to use the Quakerly silence in any constructive way. I realise now that I was asking far too much of myself, too soon.

My deep distress went unrecognised by others, mainly because of the colossal effort I made to conform to the behavioural codes surrounding the Quaker form of worship. I was acutely aware of the cultural and theological rules about how often, when, and in what way the silence may be broken, and that displays of emotion were a rarity. I already felt constricted and dissatisfied by the behavioural liturgy, and the dominance of 'weighty' Friends, to the extent that I never, ever, spoke in meeting, instead maintaining a safe passivity.

On one occasion, I recognised the onset of an anxiety attack, and went out of meeting. As I left, I told one person the reason I was leaving, and she followed me out; however, the poor Friend had absolutely no idea what to do and went into panic mode herself! She returned to the meeting and told the others; as they trooped out for coffee, some glanced at me cagily, but, since I was behaving 'normally' – sitting quietly with a glass of water – they seemed to think that they could safely ignore me.

I once tried to explain my difficulties with silence to a Friend, and I started by saying how hard it was for me, after my husband's death, each time I returned to my empty, silent house. I dreaded stepping inside, and would sit outside in the car, crying, and then I would rush inside, turning on lights, television, and radio in all the rooms, to give myself an illusion of human presence other than myself. As I began to explain my past difficulties with the silence, the Friend interrupted by saying, "Oh, but the Quaker silence is a different sort of silence". Not to me it wasn't, at the time! The Friend's well-meaning response highlighted to me the general lack of awareness of mental illness, and the sufferer's often simple need for warmth and acceptance.

My daughter suggested a very effective cure to my need for a presence in the house. She came with me to an animal shelter, where I obtained two young cats. I concentrated on their needs, and then, every time I returned to the house after shopping or whatever, I would hurry straight indoors to see what mischief the naughty moggies had been up to in my absence!

I continued to attend meeting and returned to the Anglican services of my youth. There I appreciated being 'carried' by the corporate call-and-response, as well as enjoying a rousing hymn, the physicality of ritual, listening to a good, prepared address, the chance to acknowledge my big and small screw-ups and even the provocative challenge of reciting the creed. I was interested to note that the congregation consisted of people from a wide range of backgrounds. I was beginning to develop a new assertiveness – which I feel sure was indicative of my recovery – and at that point I decided that the Quaker silence was a challenge too far, and that meeting did not meet my needs. I made a firm decision to 'de-select' myself and to resign membership. No one came to ask me why.

Fifteen years later, I have moved on and I am stronger. I attend meeting near my new home, and applied for membership. I welcome the concept of the creative, open space provided by silent worship.

I find my brain goes into sensory overload

I have a long-standing, deep-rooted, severe depressive illness. Concentration and memory problems often go with depression. A few years ago I was extremely ill and in hospital for several months. I actually managed to take an overdose when I was in hospital. I remember the consultant coming to sit next to me on the ward the day after that and asking me if I would consider ECT (electroconvulsive therapy). I agreed so had 12 treatments. Many people still do not like the idea of ECT because it used to be given abusively as well as for genuinely therapeutic reasons. Nowadays, in my experience at least, it is used with far more discrimination and sensitivity and I have seen it save lives, including mine.

Since then my overall mood, on the surface at least, has been better so in some ways I am coping better and am less of a risk to myself. However, my ability to tolerate any kind of sensory overload, especially noise or talking, is now not at all good. Because of this I have to ask people to converse in a Quakerly fashion, i.e. leaving a space between each speaker, not interrupting each other or jumping straight in with what they want to say. Of course this is not easy for people except in meetings for worship, for business, etc., where our business method is expected and used. If I cannot achieve what I need I become very distressed, which I hate anyone else seeing, so have to leave whatever is going on. It is not panic, it is a profoundly physical sensation of overload and my brain simply blowing its fuses and closing down. I feel that I have a responsibility to look after myself in those circumstances and really appreciate it when Friends can respond as I need, though I do understand when people are involved with a conversation and passionate about what they want to say. I wish that I could still take part like that myself, but I can't. I have tried explaining this to Friends by comparing it to brain injury because I find that they can understand it if there is a physical explanation rather than one related to my mental health. It is also frustrating and depressing that I can't function as they do and I'd much rather not be in a situation where this is apparent to me.

I've nearly always felt a deep emptiness

I became deeply interested in Quakers' open-minded approach to the search for divine direction and purpose.

I have been doing service-user involvement work for several years after attending a day centre for ex-psychiatric patients in my local community and learning of how to take part in different types of user involvement.

I was dual diagnosed with clinical depression and addiction issues after trying to abstain from using narcotics and suffering a mental and emotional breakdown; I had been in active addiction for 23 years. As a teenager I discovered the euphorically liberating effects of alcohol and would use it whenever I had the chance. By the time I was old enough to legally frequent pubs and clubs my love affair with alcohol was becoming problematic and I opted for drugs like cannabis and downers (sleeping pills) that seemed to give me more control and less negative consequences. By the time I discovered crack cocaine I had already been using hallucinogenic drugs regularly at illegal raves all over England. So at this time in my life it didn't seem unusual to be getting high every day.

Being in an altered state was my solution to living life on life's terms; I found it a great salve for treating resentment, fear and the perpetual feeling of differentness I had felt throughout my life. To be honest I'm not sure how I would have coped with the challenges that I was dealt in life without drugs of one kind or another and I have to say it wasn't all doom and gloom, I did have a lot of fun with them; I felt more connected and 'in the moment' when I was high and consequently found it almost effortless to deal with a variety of different (and often interesting) situations that I may have found harrowing without my chemical sustenance.

My problems began when drugs no longer seemed to treat my underlying condition, the internal condition that was always there in varying degrees and would surface without any warning; I would have days when I just couldn't shake it off no matter how many drugs were in my system. I would also try to treat this condition with a variety of other things like pornography, sex, relocations, retail therapy and even by joining and trying to get involved in things that might give me a feeling of purpose and direction like socialist parties and religious groups. But sadly the deep and enduring feeling of emptiness and despair would not go away.

This malady had been with me from as far back as I can remember. I've nearly always felt to some extent a deep emptiness and dis-connection (of varying degrees) from all those around me and this at times made it hard or nigh impossible for me to be around others, and to my utter dismay I found that when the feeling was acute it was also unbearable to be alone!

This loneliness, irritability and discontentedness would no longer recede when I used drugs and this was when at last I sought help.

I spent the next five years trying and failing to stop using narcotics and although I was less unbalanced than I was in 2002 I was unable to live life without being in an altered state, be it with cannabis, benzodiazepines, narcotics, or all three of the aforementioned. After a period in a psychiatric ward I was discharged and after a few months in the care of the home treatment team I was referred to my local Community Mental Health Team. I was referred from the Community Mental Health Team to the Munro Clinic at Guy's Hospital where I had some CAT (cognitive analytical therapy) and although I found the experience interesting and to some degree useful I was far from 'out of the woods' at this stage.

My salvation began in 2006 when it was suggested by an addiction counsellor at the Community Mental Health Team to have a look at the 12-step approach via Narcotics Anonymous where I met addicts who (actively working the 12-step programme) had found a way to stay clean by following the practical programme of action. I've been clean since 2007 thanks to the simple programme and I now help other addicts to work the 12 steps.

Not long after that I met service users at a day centre who were involved in user involvement work and seemed to benefit from the routine and purpose it gave them. Although I was in full-time work at this time I decided to attempt to do some user involvement work and started by becoming a member of a Mind User Council representing the same day centre that I regularly attended. This in time led to other user involvement opportunities and before long I was quite busy.

The combination of helping addicts and doing wide-ranging service user involvement work has given me a new purpose and vision; I now do an assortment of user involvement work with several organisations. I have to say that another major element that helps me to maintain a balance and a satisfying level of wellbeing is my Quaker membership; I became a Quaker in 2009 after attending regular meetings for about 18 months at Friends House in North West London. Even before attending regular meetings I was reading Quaker books for at least two years; I became deeply interested in their open-minded approach to the search for divine direction and purpose; I also believe in everyone having "that of God" within them and the 'inner journey' that I feel benefits from when I diligently embark on it.

Currently peer support in its various forms is my 'passion' and I have seen some encouraging outcomes from some of the work I've been involved with. Using peer support I am now running a personal development project involving mentoring that is designed to benefit people with a lived experience of enduring psychological problems. I've now been given funding to pilot this project.

I think there is much scope for the widening of the involvement initiative and I dream of the day when it becomes a fully authentic way of improving mental health services that could benefit service users, professionals, service providers and local communities.

Learning to be with a Friend who has dementia

A woman had worn out her welcome at other local churches and for months she disrupted worship and business with long tirades about social issues of the past which still preoccupied her. Elders visited to discuss. Initially we were kind and polite and got nowhere. Then we tried speaking as though to a child: simply, bluntly and firmly, telling her that she must listen in meeting for worship and not speak every time.

At the same time we encouraged her to talk endlessly and repetitively afterwards with a few patient Friends and we set up a 'discussion group' to enable her to feel heard. She has become considerably calmer, rarely speaks inappropriately and, equally important, her elderly husband is grateful for our acceptance and seems to value the hour's respite on Sunday mornings. And the discussion group continues and serves a different purpose.

Other people cannot understand the changes in me

I am a Quaker and I have an invisible disability, an Acquired Brain Injury (ABI). I got my ABI from an accident, which left me in a coma for six weeks. Because of the severity of my ABI, I am unable to hold down a job with an employer, and have memory, cognitive and emotional problems due to the frontal lobe damage to my brain.

I am, however, a walking, talking, thinking human being with a brain injury, a photographer, a writer and photographic artist.

I use photographs with written text (written by the subject of the photograph) to turn the portrait into a meaningful message. I completed a degree course where I was taught to use photographs with written text to produce meaning.

I have a book sold globally and on its second print and I am working on a second book.

I began giving voluntary photography activity sessions at homeless hostels around London. I went to a rehabilitation programme and attend specialist ABI classes for people leaving hospital following a coma or a stroke.

I do voluntary work for the Quakers, and have been working on a photographic project, trying to raise awareness of mental illness to remove the stigma associated with it.

ABI can be gained from a stroke, a fall, accident or blow to the head. You are never the same after an ABI even when you have learned to balance and walk unaided after physiotherapy sessions, been to speech therapy with the speech therapist, and you appear a normal citizen. You develop into a totally different personality type.

Other people cannot understand the changes as they are internal, cognitive, related to memory, anxiety and being slow, unaware, insensitive and self-obsessed.

My recurrent nightmare

....

The following story contains some strong images about killing. It has also been edited to remove most references to people, situations and time that may identify the author or those associated.

Sometimes I awake from sleep in the morning with my heart racing and my head buzzing. I have experienced another nightmare. A recurrent nightmare. An experience from the past which I had hoped to forget. I cannot discuss it with my fellows – even my doctor. Initially, for some years, I suffered from post-traumatic stress disorder, but at that time it was not then recognised by the medical fraternity. This condition had an effect on my job and mental attitude. Eventually, crowded out by later personal experiences, my condition became one of bipolar disorder, as diagnosed by my doctor. I am under medication. The condition is not manic, but I do have periods of acute depression, when I have difficulty in remembering and concentrating.

Whilst on active service in the armed forces many years ago, I, with several other colleagues and my closest buddy Johnny, was ordered to a dull and boring sentry duty on the back of a column of trucks en route to collect fresh supplies. It was hot and I was dozing under the tarpaulin over the back of the truck having just come off night duty. Orders are orders, and I was obliged to comply. I drew my weapon from the armaments section and reported for guard duty, a 40-mile journey along an open macadam road. The driver found every pot hole along the route. My head involuntarily slumped over my knees as I sat uncomfortably in the back of the bouncing truck. Perspiration started to ooze from every pore of my body. I dozed asleep. A sudden scream of brakes and I bundled out from the truck. I fell on the hard road surface, swearing profusely to myself.

We were in an ambush. Loud noise deafened my ears. There was an explosion up ahead, probably from a hand-made grenade, and small arms fire rattling over to my left on the south of the road. Johnny impetuously raced ahead, yelling excitedly. Bullets hit the sandy rocky ground in front of me. The enemy had my position, but not the range. I dropped down flat on the ground for cover. I reacted according to my military training. I heard yelling, another explosion from a grenade, and more small arms fire in front of me. Johnny yelled encouragement. He took the point ready to draw fire from the enemy. He stood up and starting running for cover provided by some rocks about 50 yards to his left. Ahead and to my right, a colleague gave covering fire.

There were several points of fire up ahead and to my right. About five or six terrorists were determined to make life unpleasant for us. They had an untrained yet personal determination to be rid of us. Johnny went down to my left. I knew that he had been hit. He was finished. I saw the point of fire to my right. Immediately a young terrorist broke cover and ran darting and weaving towards a copse of gnarled olive trees. I jumped up from my prone position and gave chase. It seemed to take five minutes (but in the heat of human conflict it must have been no more than a few seconds). The adrenalin was surging round my metabolism. This is why we had been trained! "You are an idiot!" I told myself. "You can't run after him and take him alive. In a moment he'll be in the sun. Then you'll not be able to see him. You're exposing yourself unnecessarily. You couldn't bring him down before he gains cover. What are you going to do if he turns and presents fire? That sun is scorching hot. This blasted Bren is getting heavier. You're thirsty! You're hungry! You're fed up and want to go home!"

I dropped down to the prone position lying on my stomach. I clipped a full magazine on top of my gun. My left index finger flipped the switch to automatic. My right index finger and thumb pulled back the cocking stud. Clearly, I saw my target in the sights. I held my breath momentarily. I hesitated a moment. Coolly and calmly I squeezed off five rounds. Even to this day I can remember glancing over the sights and seeing the top half of the terrorist's body departing company with the lower half, and moving off in a different direction.

The small arms fire ceased as abruptly as it had started. My colleagues behind me and to my right had crept up and gunned down the remaining terrorists. We took stock of the situation. Johnny was dead. Shot clean through the side of his head. My man was in two pieces some ten yards apart. He was dead.

There were no further casualties to our group. We dragged the bodies to the roadside, and left them to be collected by troops following us. I was sweating profusely. My knees suddenly started to give way and I felt wobbly.

Hours later, when we had returned back to camp and reported the incident to the Security Officer, I was horribly physically sick. I felt that way for two days after. It was my first kill. The boys back at camp welcomed me as a hard tough guy. The bullies would no longer pick on me. I missed Johnny. He was dead. I had let him down badly.

Years after this event, I remember the sight of my man falling into two pieces before my deadly accurate fire. I remember also that I had hesitated to open fire. I blame myself for some religious scruple which had cost Johnny's life. If I had opened fire earlier, then Johnny would have lived. I had hesitated, and that rests on my conscience. I have told very few people of this incident. Nobody would believe me anyway.

I seem to recollect that there were three considerations to this encounter.

- I had hesitated to open fire. My scruples had cost Johnny's life. If I had opened fire earlier would he have lived?
- I had actually taken a life – in contravention of the Ten Commandments.
- The most sinister aspect of this encounter was the fact that I had actually enjoyed killing this terrorist.

The matter has given me nightmares and depression sporadically ever since.

I was accepted into membership of the Religious Society of Friends in the mid-1990s. The fellowship, tranquillity, ministry all combined to help me and alleviate current periods of depression. I do what I can, when I can, and if I can to help others on the road ahead. My ministry is accepted. People like me and I seem to fit into the spirit of the occasion.

For me, being a Quaker is better than my medication.

Trying to be inclusive...

About a year ago an elderly man started attending our meetings for worship. He tends to arrive early and stand at the library shelf in the hallway where he picks up a publication and proceeds to read it out loud. At about the right time, he enters the meeting room and he sits down, always in the same place which is a far corner away from anybody else. He always picks up a Bible or *Quaker faith & practice* and reads quietly to himself through the meeting. He makes quite a lot of noise some of the time, loudly enough to be audible to everyone else in the meeting. Three quarters of the way through the meeting he will often stand and minister, always very briefly and always along the lines of "I pray for the perfection of redemption, in the name of Jesus Christ".

After meeting for worship he often leaves during notices, rather than when we are shaking hands or when notices have finished. He never engages in conversation, or stays for a cup of tea, or ever attends any of our other events.

Many of us have tried to converse with him but with no response. We hoped he might join the 'circle' of the meeting but he resolutely sits in the corner. One or two Friends make a point of going and shaking his hand at the end of meeting. Once after meeting when he was particularly noisy one of us spoke to him and asked him if he was OK because he had been making a lot of noise. "Oh, was I?", he said.

Peace was restored

Some years ago there was a young man who unexpectedly began to be very disruptive in our Quaker meeting. He had come to Quakers several years before from a strict, biblical and evangelical sect.

His disruptive behaviour took the form of haranguing us, especially with biblical texts during meeting for worship, arguing with our processes within meeting and especially in meeting for business. He disputed the accuracy of minutes of meetings he had not attended and if he was at meeting for business he was negative and argumentative. The meeting was very troubled. Various members tried reasoning with him by talking and in writing. Eventually and with much concern he was asked not to come to meeting for business. A friend sat outside with him. We did have a contingency plan if he was disruptive and the meeting was very relieved that we did not have to use it.

One Sunday during meeting for worship he harangued us at length quoting biblical passages that "proved our sinfulness" and finished by calling us fascists. In the ensuing silence one of our young Friends, a young woman of 13 or 14, stood and with tears in her eyes said, "I don't know what a fascist is but I know I am not one" and sat down. Our disturbed Friend walked across the room, hugged her and returned to his seat.

Peace was restored.

Some weeks later a friend happened to see him at the hospital in the waiting room of the Mental Health Unit. We did not really realise that he had mental health issues at the time of all the disturbance until being seen there.

He came back to meeting and was part of it.

At another meeting we have had a similar occurrence though not quite as disruptive and again we did not realise that there were mental health issues until the disturbance was 'resolved', this time by the person (and spouse) asking to be removed from membership and all other contact with Quakers.

It seems to me from these two encounters that we may miss the fact that there are mental health issues and interpret the problems to a person just being difficult.

Eventually I had a breakdown

I went to Yearly Meeting in Canterbury in August 2011 but was already sinking. I was struggling to eat enough and sleeping for few hours each night. I kept myself to myself for much of the time, feeling quite alone even with so many people around. I went with my friend to the Quaker Life session about mental health in meetings but don't remember much, although I do remember knowing that it was important.

On return and into the autumn of 2011 I went to meeting on various occasions, getting involved with some music making with the children but struggling to keep hold of my emotions. I told one or two Friends a little of what was happening to me and of my past (child sexual abuse) but although there was some support such as counselling sessions with a Friend with experience of this and visiting another Friend's house several times to cry, I would have benefited from more proactive support.

Eventually I had a breakdown, following which I was unable to go anywhere by myself. I now had the involvement of various mental health professionals, anti-psychotic medication and a private therapist, initially funded with support from a couple of very special people. During this difficult time I was unbelievably still able to work. This was due to having a non-demanding job working with busy children who distracted me from myself. And as I was unable to cope with 'myself' by myself this was a workable option.

However, I sadly could no longer go to meeting… reasons as follows:
- Meeting was and is such a precious place to me, it is my second home and I therefore could not keep the emotions at bay while I was there. I was overwhelmed by them and did not know how to manage them.
- I was feeling such self-loathing and lack of self-worth that I assumed others would think the same of me so could not ask for support directly. (I thought I had hinted at my need for support by saying to someone how everyone rallied round to visit a Friend in hospital, or who was frail and needed visiting at home, but not a healthy-looking middle-aged woman who appeared on the surface to be 'fine'.)
- I did not feel that my concept, my sense of and my understanding of my God existed any longer. I was so trapped by my own overwhelming selfishness that I couldn't really care about 'God'. He just complicated thoughts in my already confused and desperate mind.
- I did not care about anyone else or anything else. I did not want to hear ministry about anyone else's problems or needs as my own were too all-encompassing.

I am much better now; but not completely. I still have vulnerabilities and 'issues' but I have come so far. I am able to sit here as I am quietly in the library writing this without crying. I am able to say hello to people, I am able to achieve eye contact and I am starting to be interested in the rest of the world again.

That is how and why I am able to write this now.

The following is a list of what support I wish that I could have had from Friends in the meeting:

- Phone calls, emails, messages, cards, visits… I was ill after all!
  More persistence and proactive-ness with the above… just because I didn't respond when someone did get in touch didn't mean I didn't value the contact. It just meant I was too ill to respond.
- Invitations to events, a meal out, a concert, being part of a friendship group. Perhaps one day I could have gone. At least offers would have made sure I knew I was being thought about.
- Perhaps some regular updates with what was happening in the meeting, so I didn't miss the kind of news that engenders a sense of belonging in a group, such as deaths, births, marriages.
- A named Friend to 'look after me' when I was able or wanting to come to meeting. They could have met me at the door. I could have sat next to them, they could have acted as an intermediary when people asked me questions and I couldn't respond, they could have been ready with the tissues to settle me in a quiet corner when it all became too much. They would have understood without my needing to spell it out, that at meeting I felt like a young frightened girl inside and wanted/needed to be treated as such.
- Hugs, hugs and more hugs. For me physical contact, once so abhorrent, now reminds me that I am human, cared for… dare I say loved by others and that means so much to me.

Maybe someone can understand the psychology of all that, I'm not sure I can although I do know that it is something to do with meeting for worship being my 'home' and that I want to be safe here and looked after when I am vulnerable and above all I want to be wholly 'myself' here and not pretending to be well and strong and OK if I am not.

I finish with a very big thank you to those Friends who have been there for me and helped me through including doing some of the above.

I don't want any of the above to be taken as criticism of any one or group of people. It is simply my experience put into written words so that it may help others to understand.

Light or dark?

In a review of the meeting, a question was asked was about 'light and light groups'. In response, I commented that some years ago in the North East of England a group was formed, from various faith traditions, on the theme of 'dark holy ground', in response to industrial decline and unemployment and consequent problems such as stress and depression. This approach seems to me to make far more sense, and to be far more sensitive, than banging on about 'light'.

At worst I would have killed myself

I was diagnosed with clinical depression and treated accordingly but was later re-diagnosed as bipolar. I've been on mood stabilisers for some time. It's taken its toll in broken relationships; not being able to work full time; and creating havoc from time to time. On the up side I built and then sold a business with 100 employees. I manage my own condition largely outside the NHS (apart from meds) and see recovery as a lifetime and daily time-consuming journey. Like many people with chronic mental health conditions I'm an expert patient – particularly on recovery. I have an understanding of the additional pressures faced by gay men who often present with problems.

I have had a great deal of support from individual Friends who also have mental health conditions – they are my buddy system. I've also been able to support them. The first was my Seroxat buddy (the drugs I was on then). I was able to 'come out' with a mental health problem to a few people, and quickly found someone in the same boat in my meeting who helped me for a few years until I moved meetings. I have found similar support in two other meetings – my peer group support. I would always seek help first from a fellow Quaker. I could not have survived without my buddy. At worst I would have killed myself but without her I know I would have been hospitalised several times.

It requires people to be honest in their own meeting about their condition and seeing if someone pops up as a potential buddy. The buddy is there at the end of a phone as well as for real – not least to encourage each other to keep going to meeting when social interaction seems impossible. This is not a substitute for therapy – but very practical, down-to-earth, old-fashioned help.

I am against 'training' of overseers. It is a minefield. Mental health is so varied and we tend to be experts on our condition and don't want someone to 'share my pain' or try to come up with solutions (which is often meds). But I do need some people in my meeting to understand that I have an ongoing condition.

One problem is that Quakers feel they have to 'do something' where often we simply need encouragement to come to meeting. It is helpful for other people to understand that we may seem very distant at times, for all sorts of reasons, or that for many our energy flags and we may go to ground for a while and so on but we don't want to be forgotten. Ideally we want to have contact with other Quakers with similar problems. A reminder about getting outside help is so important.

A big thing certainly is to help meetings draw the line when they are out of their depth and to point them in the right direction for help. Of course there are going to be people who disrupt the meeting and make life impossible for everyone else. Trying to understand the problems of a paranoid schizophrenic is impossible for the layperson and meetings need to be supported in looking at the problem – not as a mental health problem that they will never solve (so stop trying to help) but deal with it as you would with other disruptive behaviour. Quaker meeting is not respite care or a refuge for the very ill. It may sound harsh but if we want to be treated as someone with an illness – all the same rules apply. I should not be allowed to come to meeting if I have an infectious disease – so why should I be allowed to come and create havoc and have sympathy because I have a mental problem.

I bumped into two people who I have not seen for years, from two separate meetings, who know I have a chronic condition. They both poured out their worries about individuals with mental health problems who were spoiling meeting for worship regularly and were frankly almost at their wits' end not knowing how to proceed. They thought that they had to 'do something Quakerly'. Well, they can't prescribe the medication which may be the only solution. They need someone to phone who has experience in mental health and will give them permission to ban them, while hopefully pointing the individual to appropriate help en route. It's a tough world.

My single best bit of advice to all of us is to keep it simple. Do nothing that creates too many expectations of an individual or could create too much work or too much stress. In other words stop acting like a 'typical Quaker'! We can be very fragile – despite appearances.

A supportive group is needed

I would like to share the experience of being involved with a person with dementia who came to my meeting. Later I found out that someone else found the experience very depressing and with hindsight realise the meeting should have been asked for support and help. Neither of us had partners or family who lived close. The person with the mental health issues was in the same position. I would like to send out a message to meetings to be alert to this situation and especially how quickly it can deteriorate and how a supportive group is needed for all concerned.

For those responsible for the right conduct and well-being of meetings

The seemingly bizarre and uncontrolled behaviour of sufferers can present a real challenge, however sympathetic one is to the individual concerned.

Conversely those afflicted with often invisible symptoms of mental disease, malaise or distress, all of which can often go on for what seems an intolerable time, often stay away from meeting for fear of adverse response from other Friends. If their condition is not known it can seem as though they have lost interest in the meeting and are not followed up for fear (among overseers) of seeming pushy.

The real issue is not people's mental health but the reaction of others who may be dismayed or downright terrified as a result of odd behaviours manifested. I don't believe that the best training pack in the world can teach people to be sensitive, tender, loving and forbearing. Loss of memory, mental infirmity and so on are more prevalent in the elderly. I think sharing stories is the *only* way to be effective. At Yearly Meeting in York it was the 'real' stories of same-sex couples with or without children and those who had made later childless marriages which made Friends think more widely around a topic to see how an apparently insoluble problem could be accommodated.

Local meeting support group

....

Addressing the challenge of mental health in meetings, we continue to offer a group for those concerned about their own mental health or that of those they care for. This has not really addressed at all the need as we perceived it, in that for the most part those with active problems, whether their own or that they are caring for someone, prefer to share this with individuals rather than a group. However, we do now have the resource of a well-established group with a wide range of experiences, which is good for participants and a contribution to the meeting's oversight, which also includes individual overseers and circles.

On trying to understand anorexia nervosa: a carer's perspective

I didn't really know anything. Despite being surrounded by news items about problems with eating and body size, and despite attending a girls' school, I managed to know practically nothing about eating disorders – until I had to learn, very quickly, in a crisis, because a member of my family got one. Suddenly I was a carer, desperately seeking information.

It seems bizarre now. Eating disorders are all around. They've been on the increase for decades. How could I not have noticed, learned something useful, done something? I think my ignorance stemmed from fear. Also from a lack of interest. I'm not proud of that, but perhaps a fairly straightforward, positive relationship with food inoculated me a little. However, I realised something quite quickly that surprised me: eating disorders are not all about food.

Perhaps my political decision not to respond to every anxiety-inducing media message, advert, or article about what women should look like, was both a deterrent to getting informed and a protective influence. But when I was growing up there weren't the pressures of social media and no such thing as websites, let alone ones actually promoting anorexia – yes, these horrors exist. Another thing I learned quickly is: it's not all about media messages either.

After hearing the terrifying diagnosis of anorexia, I even discovered there were eating disorders I didn't know existed. Of course I had heard of anorexia and bulimia. But I found out there's a catch-all acronym for all the conditions that didn't quite fit categories: EDNOS. Eating Disorders Not Otherwise Specified. What a great way of making "don't know" sound like "we've got it sussed".

Then there was the danger of letting it all get overwhelming in another way. Somewhere I read that ours is "an eating disordered society". Free markets insisting on over-consumption while giving mixed messages about the effects, guilt, restriction... was this part of a global challenge – too big to tackle? I felt defeated on several levels at once.

Returning to what was in front of me, I sought the explanation I needed, and guidance on how to manage, how to help. But each of the common myths about causes burst in the glare of first-hand experience. *Dieting gone a bit far?* That didn't tell me anything about subtleties of thought and feeling I was observing, or the changes in perception – how can a person believe themselves to be huge when they are underweight? Well, they can. *Trauma?* It seemed to be another catch-all term. I had noticed that this can mean different things to different people. Abuse as a universal cause was a supposition I'd lazily picked up before all this started, and now it was obvious this wasn't true either. *Perfectionist personality?* Well, my child was keen on writing neatly but wasn't fussed about her messy maths. It seemed a generalisation too.

So how could I get to grips with this condition – these conditions? How could I help? Suddenly I was looking after a child with a serious condition that was going rapidly out of control, which seemed ironic, because the wish for 'control' is often given as a key element in eating disorders. And eating disorders aren't all about control either. In fact, the first thing I learned was that they are about a tangle of different things. The best thing to do was start from not knowing, ditch the whys and simply work out what to do.

There were useful books about what to do, practical approaches, what not to do, although they were sometimes hard to digest after a tiring day. The resistance and repetitions were exhausting, dispiriting. Thankfully a family therapist said to us loudly and clearly "Families don't cause eating disorders". These five small words were like gold dust.

Some discoveries were a revelation. Like just how powerful thoughts and feelings can be. They can endow an under-nourished body with the physical strength of a prize fighter. Or how the mind can shut off conversation and human connection like a steel trap and (almost) convince you that the bond between you and the one you are caring for has turned to dust. How intensity of feeling about eating and food can hit your own guts and pull and tug and fling them about like a doll in the wild tentacles of a sea monster. How it's hard to keep calm and carry on. How it really matters that people club together and try to be strong as a team to help the sufferer.

Increasing understanding: possibilities

I gradually started finding some signposts, none definitive, but at least some helpful guidelines. Eating disorders are all around and nearby. Anorexia affects about one in 20 teenagers. You can get it at virtually any age – it is less likely than when you are a teenager, but not impossible. You can get it if you are a boy. A man. A girl. A woman. People with eating disorders say that the stigma and discrimination surrounding their mental health problem can be one of the hardest parts in their day-to-day experience. Currently, it is estimated that one tenth of people with an eating disorder sadly die from it or related effects. It is possible to recover completely from eating disorders. They are treatable conditions.

I also gathered some understanding about what eating disorders are NOT, which helped orientate me as I cared. They are not all about food, body image, feelings and thoughts, though these are all a very important part of the picture. They are not all about a diet gone wrong, a lifestyle choice or relationships. They are probably caused by a combination of things: possibly genetics, possibly brain function alteration (possibly caused by antibodies, or chemical reactions), possibly personality traits, environmental stress, cultural conditions, hormones, developmental transitions. Once they are established, they affect parts of the self, body, brain, emotions or thoughts. Undernourishment alters neural pathways in the brain. It's a bit like a ploughed field – much harder to plough in different lines once the furrows are channelled into the earth.

Neuroscientists are starting to understand how the brain, the mind and the body interrelate. Some geneticists are looking at genes as a contributing factor. Some persistent healthcare planners are grappling with how to plan (never mind pay for) the nationwide sustainable long-term care that eating disorders require. Meanwhile, nurses, parents, siblings, friends, are doing the day-to-day hard work of helping people with eating disorders keep nourished – with food, yes, and with other things too.

Touchstones

So, after many months of struggle and difficult mealtimes when I had not a spare neuron to think of anything except for the next spoonful and whether it was going to get eaten – I came to some very basic touchstones that helped. I found that it was important to maintain structure, and connections with others, and to care for myself, in order to hold at bay a great tsunami of need and anxiety, in order to be a carer.

I came to appreciate how deep and intricate the mind and human consciousness is. I learned to start from nothing and work from there. Take nothing for granted. Fighting won't work. A firm, gentle persistence is better. Some kind of trust was essential.

Friends and relatives offering their kindness and simple acts signalling understanding and compassion had a huge effect. That rippled to other members of the family and to our unwell child too. There is something profoundly moving in encountering human solidarity and determination to help others in distress. I'm talking about carers, parents, professionals, yes. I'm also talking about the people struggling with the eating disorders. What strength and determination it takes to find a way through towards life and nourishment, in the face of extreme feelings of fear and self-loathing, and in spite of gaps in knowledge and resources!

Friendship, acting communally, communicating well, not accepting the status quo, striving for better conditions in communities and society, speaking out, and seeing "that of God in everyone" become not just *values* but solid, robust things, lifelines that enable people to navigate vast challenges. There is much that we don't know, and much to learn about eating disorders, but starting from these basic, simple human principles seems a good way to begin.

Keeping open communication

We have had several experiences of quite extreme cases but feel we cannot make generalisations as each case is individual. Keeping open communication within the meeting and with eldership and oversight and remaining true to Quaker principles is the best foundation for managing these situations, whilst being mindful of those Friends who might be deterred from attending meeting.

I muddled through

I muddled through an uneventful career – a back-room grafter rather than a clinical leader. With the taboo that still surrounds the profession I was in and my own puffed-up pride was a kind of conspiracy to stop me getting the mental health support I needed. I had little or no informal support network. As is often the case the illness takes away one's self-awareness – I lacked anyone who was able to observe and whose advice I would take. It is so very hard for someone with mania to accept something might be wrong with *them* – paranoia tends to rule… *it's everybody else*!

Educated at an excellent Quaker school which I loved, I flirted with going to meeting occasionally in the years following… I wonder what things would have been like if I was more truly able to step off my ticking time bomb and join a Quaker fellowship somewhere, if I had begun to make a personal transformation back then. I had confused tacky entertainment and peak experiences, thrills and chemical euphoria for spiritual experience. If God was calling, I wasn't listening; he was going to have to shout a lot louder. It had become time for the shock and awe.

My career suddenly ended one afternoon while I was at my desk and the reception put through a call from a police detective. Behind the scenes my life had already gone into social, economic, behavioural and existential meltdown. By the time my boss had taken me aside about 'irritability' and suggested treatment, my life was already out of control. And in this context of course I had nightmares my job would come to an end – a job I couldn't say I exactly enjoyed – these might now be termed less nightmares and more 'wish-fulfilment', a wish to be delivered from the crazy roller-coaster, a wish for it all to stop.

After a conviction for my gross misconduct as my life was going into meltdown, after being placed onto the sex offenders register, after a move to be with a new partner, now after learning to live with long-term unemployment, after finding a new and rewarding way of life in Christianity and Quakerism, after getting on to a good new combination treatment for bipolar disorder, after being clear of drugs for more than a couple of years now, after ongoing psychological input, after regular work with a lovely probation officer, after and because of all of this, I'm a lot better. My environment has now changed so much for the better I reckon I haven't been as well since my illness began over 20 years ago. Still the illness has not gone, I do struggle with low moods, but I seem to be able to find my way out of them easier nowadays.

I have met with problems within Quakers with respect to my conviction – despite the way illness was linked – it's a bit like a glass half-full or half-empty – reassurance can be taken that while I'm well then my conduct is OK, but it's also seen that all I have to do is to get unwell and… and as Isobel Lane said, "fear is very powerful". It seems that I only pose a threat to people who don't know me, yet they are also the people in a position to give me employment and so a sense of worth in the world. I am sore after being rejected for a volunteer position with Friends. I was deemed apparently competent to do the job (and I was sure I could), it was just I posed a 'risk'. It seems to me sometimes that Quakers like to sing loudly about working in prisons, about the heritage of fair treatment of the mentally ill (I have benefited from the Retreat Hospital once myself), but to have ex-offenders or the mentally unwell actually within the Society – in meetings for worship, or doing Quaker work – well that's another matter.

You might say I'm extremely ambivalent though, because I also love the Society of Friends! It's been Friends who have helped me regain some self-respect, local Friends who have found me a number of little roles that let me feel valued. I have been able to reconfigure a trauma of losing so much in a material sense to freedom of being able to embrace a much simpler, more manageable lifestyle with Quakers, where possible together and alone to focus on the priorities of a life with God, and of love for one another. The quote by Stephen Amos (see page 66) sums up my position regarding confidentiality now: I do want to be "honest and visible". Above all, personally I hope to be able to turn a negative and still painful experience of rejection by Friends into something that leaves me feeling rather loved and valued rather than feared and mistrusted.

How do we support the caring Friends, too?

Our meeting has a Friend of long standing and so we feel a duty of care towards her. How do we support the caring Friends, too?

She is a childless widow, more or less bed-bound and very confused. One of our overseers has organised her life for her and has become indispensable to her well-being; this overseer is often away and then other Friends, less available, are obliged to step in. She does not appreciate the substitution and can be sharp-tongued.

One Friend's stories

She told me she had a psychiatric problem which showed itself as a sudden shout which she was not necessarily aware of. I said I would sit with her and meantime debated whether to tell the elders and overseers, which I did eventually. Unfortunately her shout happened when I wasn't there and she was approached and 'spoken to' by another Friend!

Recently we have had an attender – a man in his mid-fifties – who told me he has Asperger's Syndrome. For a long time he wouldn't give us any details other than his first name, but gradually he told us a bit about himself. To cut a long story short, he is now a regular attender, friendly and has given ministry. I feel our meeting has helped him and his family think the same, but it has been a long and patient process. It was a help that he told us of his condition. As I write I am conscious that I have labelled him but I know that he is now 'Anthony' with no label.

Some time ago, a close friend of mine took her own life. She was a doctor and a psychiatrist and had suffered from depression for very many years. Not long ago my daughter took me to her grave. I had had the stone cleaned and my daughter read out the letters after her name – four lots of four in all. She turned to me and said, "Mum, that's what we should dwell on – all she achieved and not what happened at the end."

A former attender had been sectioned and was in the local psychiatric hospital. She and her partner were with us a few years ago. She had a spell in the hospital then during which time she was accused of throwing a cup of coffee over a male nurse. Fortunately we knew the chaplain at the hospital who was a tremendous help. Eventually there were three court cases and on each occasion she was supported by the chaplain and three or four other Friends. She was acquitted. It was interesting that as soon as I telephoned the chaplain (not knowing the name of the nurse in question), his reply was, "I can guess who the nurse was". She and her female partner were articulate, intelligent and compassionate. However, there were times when they acted and dressed differently. They moved to two other places within our area meeting and each time received great support from local Friends. We are still in touch as are the Friends who helped them previously.

Does everyone have a family or neighbours to support them?

I had noticed already some confusion and loss of memory in one Friend from our meeting so we were not surprised to hear that she had been diagnosed with Alzheimer's – though she seemed not really to accept the implications of the disease. Apparently she told her GP that she had no kin.

Since I had known her the longest, I was the elder who attended the local Dementia Awareness Group (intended for carers) on behalf of the meeting. The Friend had told me that the GP wouldn't help her, so I contacted a dementia adviser who was available once a week at the doctor's surgery (incidentally, the receptionists were unaware of this and at first denied his existence, which highlighted the difficulty that people might have accessing the service). Eventually I met the adviser and told him that this Friend felt unsupported after her diagnosis. He investigated and discovered that she had failed to keep several appointments made with mental health practitioners although this was never followed up; it is assumed that every patient has family or neighbours to remind them. I was shocked. Don't they recognise that some people will have severe memory problems?

She had also refused to accept whatever help had been offered by Social Services. Friends in our meeting are kind and tried to respond in their own ways to her complaints of loneliness. She has been single and fiercely independent all her life and dismisses what she regards as inappropriate offers of help or visits with bruising brusqueness: "I'm not daft or helpless, you know!" So Friends retire hurt.

Some Friends have got drawn in...

An attender at our meeting is from another Christian tradition. She is not very interested in Quakerism but she knew some nice Quakers in her childhood and so took to coming to us on Sundays. She has little family support and I feel that she is lonely and plays one Friend off against another. Some Friends have got sucked into playing a very large role in organising her finances and care arrangements.

Our meeting is experiencing great challenges

How to convey to social workers, mental health professionals and to GPs who won't listen, the fact that a Quaker meeting is *not* a social care agency, nor a mental health drop-in centre, nor a legal advocate (although informally, in practice we offer some of all of this, as I suspect all meetings do). Also that it is unreasonable to expect us to replace family support where it does not exist as we have no authority to intervene. We ourselves understand the need to draw up Power of Attorney documents but often it is too late and in any case probably not appropriate for a Friends' meeting to accept this responsibility.

The problems can be compounded by elders and overseers acting individually as well as by other well-meaning Friends who have become over-involved themselves. When they feel overstretched themselves or go on holiday, they look to others in the meeting, who may feel less capable, or reluctant, to pick up the involvement. This generates divisiveness, bad feelings and a sense of failure.

A few of us who have worked with social services and mental health teams understand the boundaries of this work and the dangers of overreaching amateurs, but other Friends, who may be used to professional authority but lack relevant experience, see it as our Quaker duty to respond to calls for help, regardless of our own advancing age and lack of up-to-date skills.

Our membership includes a Friend prone to bouts of severe depression, which does not disturb our worship but exhausts his partner who needs help to endure the situation without over reacting.

Our collective time is greatly taken up with the problems of a few older Friends at the expense of others and activities the meeting might be undertaking. We wish to steer other meetings facing similar situations away from the pitfalls we have encountered.

I have a head injury

I have a head injury acquired from a motorcycle accident. I gained great comfort and have learned fresh 'coping strategies' from reading the book *A New Earth: Awakening to Your Life's Purpose* by Eckhart Tolle, who writes that you are not your thinking mind, your desire or your fear, you are the perceiver of them.

I find that in a Quaker meeting, one can escape the thinking mind into a space where you are open to the reality of time and space; your breathing, the sensation of your heartbeat and the presence of others beyond yourself – a silent connection with the meeting, essentially escaping the ego voice inside your head into an experience of external reality – with others.

Feelings of guilt

I come from a family where mental health was not mentioned or acknowledged, giving rise, in my case anyway, to feelings of guilt.

My depression began at boarding school. Fifteen years later, with three small children and a difficult marriage, I asked for medical help.

Later I went to college and trained as a primary school teacher. I acquired my own home by becoming a part-time meeting house caretaker/warden alongside teaching. The following year, due to continual ill health and the recurrence of depression I had a breakdown.

After four months off work and now regularly seen by a psychiatrist I went back to teaching but after two years I was forced to retire due to 'mental and physical inability to cope'.

The indoor and outdoor maintenance and upkeep of the meeting house and gardens was a 'lifesaver'!

I also attended yoga classes.

I lived alone and rarely saw Friends except, of course, on Sunday – and had no close neighbours.

Asked repeatedly on Sunday mornings "How are you?" I couldn't say "I am fine" if I wasn't and this led to more questions. When depression was mentioned there was little sympathy or understanding apart from a Friend who was invaluable in spite of never encountering depression before. She was wonderful!

The meeting generally seemed to have no understanding and shied away from contact especially during the week. As the warden I lived on the job and had to be on hand most of the time whether or not I was suffering from depression.

Eventually I discovered a local programme called 'The Outlook Recovery Plan – Fight Depression and Win'. The psychiatrist I saw regularly encouraged me to get involved – it was a life-saver and is still a part of my daily life.

I retired in 2001 and now live with my family – I have 'a granny flat'.

Looking back on my years of entwined wardenship and depression I think misunderstanding of the illness, recognition that it *is* an illness and the difficulty so many people have in confronting it is the cause of much of the problem. A person looks well so people think "What is the matter with you?"!

Two situations involving depression

I've dealt with two situations involving mental health, both cases of depression. My wife is a chronic depressive. Her periodic breakdowns were very hard on me as well as on her. My meeting tried to be supportive, but the effect was that people always started by asking how she was as soon as any encounter took place, and I was totally marginalised: I was 'The Person with the Depressive Wife Problem'.

Recently I've had a serious depressive breakdown myself and have for nearly a year been on anti-depressants. I believe it was because of a very serious clash with a friend. I didn't want to be 'The Person Suffering from Depression', so I said nothing about it to anyone in the meeting. This has worked reasonably well, I think – except it has meant that I can't tell anyone about the upsetting circumstances of the breakdown, which might have helped. However, I have help from the medical profession for that. But it seems a bit of a pity that it's impossible to share things like this with members of my meeting without risking its taking over everyone's consciousness. Preferring to be treated as a person, not a problem, I've got 'enough' of what I want for it to have worked out as well as it can.

In general, Friends seem often to put on too concerned an attitude, as if attending a Great Tragedy, when the sufferer really wants to be cheered up and treated normally. I've seen this with people dying as well.

I needed support

I was living in a new place where I knew no one and my husband was starting a new demanding job. My son was born and welcomed by the overseers at the meeting to which I had just transferred my membership. I succumbed to acute post-natal depression necessitating hospitalisation. Friends in the meeting were at a loss. The meeting offered to pick me up from the hospital for meeting for worship but this was too much of an ordeal. I only went once. I must have seemed difficult and ungrateful but what I really needed was the constant, undemanding support of an individual.

The local vicar's wife took in my husband and son and brought the baby to visit me regularly. Her kindness stays with me and motivated me to work with mentally distressed people.

Eventually I came through and resumed going to meeting, but Friends did not refer to the reason for my long absence. I think they were embarrassed. I could have done with a sympathetic ear.

"Oh, I go to the Quakers now. They'll look after me"

I saw a neighbour in my village who had told me of their recent diagnosis with Alzheimer's disease. I had helped them to move. I heard them say to a woman who had asked how they were managing: "Oh, I go to the Quakers now. They'll look after me". I alerted my fellow elders and overseers to this misconception of the meeting's role and opinion was divided. The two of us who had worked in the field of mental health cautioned against hasty over-involvement. Since there was a diagnosis we felt it was imperative to work with and through the mental health professionals, gingering them up when necessary. Other members of the meeting however, relying too much on the curative power of tea and chat for this worsening condition, sadly added to the confusion by overwhelming the person with alternative suggestions without knowing all the facts. Elders and overseers agreed that I should liaise with her family and the GP. I felt that I was acting as a 'Quakerly' individual but not 'on behalf of the meeting' since we are not equipped or qualified to cope with such a responsibility.

The person attended regularly for a year and a half and then, when they'd been absent for several weeks, I called to make sure they were all right. They said that as they lived alone and never saw anyone to talk to they didn't need any more silence and wouldn't be coming again. I confess to a feeling of relief, as an elder.

It felt as if I had been blown apart

I was devastated by a murder in my family. It felt as if I had been blown apart and splattered on the walls.

It took a very long time to scrape the bits off the wall into a congealed heap to form a limp rag in the corner of the room, and even longer to get back on my knees, never mind back up on my feet. I did not know the effects of a traumatic bereavement, nor did my meeting, and I coasted along on autopilot (including in Quaker roles) until finally running out of steam.

It felt as if Friends found it inconvenient that it took me more than a few weeks, never mind years, to begin to recover. There was no funeral for eight weeks; a nearly three-year wait for a trial with postponements and cancellations en route; and a further year before publication of the Independent Mental Health Inquiry.

Participating in an Escaping Victimhood retreat went some way to 'putting Humpty-Dumpty together again'. However, I still find my 'internal wiring' is not secure and shorts out under stress. Small things cause a large upset and take a long recovery time. I am not returned to being the strong person I was 'before'.

For my meeting, I feel that it was disconcerting for them to find a person changed without obvious physical cause from an active member to a drop-out, and then back to not wholly dependable participation. In my experience, Friends do not see the 'emotional wheelchair' under their own noses.

Learning from experiences

We hope that, should we encounter problems of mental health in the future, we shall have the confidence to know what, as a meeting, we can do and what is beyond our remit. Friends will trust their elders and overseers to take appropriate action on behalf of the meeting. My own experience inclines me to think that a designated Friend (not necessarily an elder or overseer) known to the sufferer should give them help. They will need the gifts of patience and understanding and ideally experience; this Friend should be given the support and trust of the meeting.

I needed space

I had a depressive breakdown, and was unable to continue to work. Although I had left my home, I had to return to live and be cared for by my elderly mother.

I was in my thirties and had spent several years abroad, returning to undertake a specialist teaching course. I was undergoing psychotherapy treatment three times per week, paid for privately.

A member of the Quaker meeting where I had been a member was asked to contact me, which she did by phone. She pressed me to let her visit. I tried to explain that I did not wish her to come, but she repeated her request. As a result I felt the only way I could stop her was to resign my membership of the society, which I did.

Fortunately, after I had fully recovered and had moved elsewhere, I again applied for membership and have continued to take up an active part in my local and area meetings.

I hope this may point out the necessity for being sensitive to our members' feelings.

Seeking support

How quickly everything can fall apart. I'm the mother of a son who has, for some years, suffered from bouts of anxiety and depression. Since he's living at home I am by default the carer.

Although he seems to have coped well with his current course, and I believe he enjoys it, he had a week, just when he was supposed to be finishing his written course work and preparing for exams, when he was struggling to such an extent he just went to bed and gave up completely. Luckily this only lasted for a week and he seems to have got back on his feet and fired into action.

It was very distressing for me (and I'm sure it was for him) as I realised how quickly everything can fall apart, and I'm uncertain what to do to help him for the best at these extremely challenging times.

He cannot admit that he is ill and refuses to use any of the support services that are available to him through the university. He seems unwilling or unable to discuss his feelings at home or elsewhere.

He has become solitary and spends all his time at home alone in his room, despite the fact that when he's with some members of the family he becomes very gregarious.

His lack of self-confidence seems to overwhelm him without realising what's going on.

My experience of being a carer is sometimes frightening, at not understanding what's going on or how to support my son effectively. This becomes exhausting and draining.

I would welcome meeting up with others who have similar experiences and sharing ways of supporting each other.

I am bipolar

A few years ago I went through a period of being quite depressed and so I stopped attending meeting for worship even though I had been attending quite regularly.

Out of the blue I received in the post a card signed by people at meeting saying they hoped I was OK.

I was touched by this and thought it was the sign of a caring community.

Overseers' reflections

It is important to get to know the person and their circumstances, remembering that Friends are generally not meddlesome.

It may be right to seek professional help but this could be problematic if we are unsure of someone's mental health.

There is a bigger umbrella than mental health.

What about a temporary crisis? Is it a common experience that Quakers put too much pressure on a Friend so he or she can't properly operate?

Any one of us might be mentally unstable at times.

We need to see the person in a particular setting, affected by the particular members around.

As you can see, there is a problem defining parameters and therefore we find it difficult to offer specific examples.

One meeting's awareness

When we hear the outer door open after the beginning of meeting for worship, we go out and if it is this particular attender we sit and talk to him outside and if possible dissuade him from going into the children's meeting, in another room. We accompany him if he insists on going in there. Giving this individual attention by talking to him often seems to help him when he eventually comes into the meeting for worship. This doesn't work always, as it depends on his state that day.

A man quietly weeping

I was sitting in an unaccustomed seat and noticed a man quietly weeping throughout the meeting and was surprised that no one responded to this. When I spoke to an elder he explained that no one knew the man but that he was brought occasionally by a nurse from the local mental hospital. I made a point of speaking to them and the nurse spoke enthusiastically of the benefit gained by his patient from the experience. He asked, perhaps inappropriately, if he might bring others "to profit from the therapy". Elders decided, perhaps rightly, that such a group might threaten the quality and integrity of worship for others and the request was declined. I don't know whether there was any discussion about this with the hospital.

Seeking a deeper understanding

How interesting and necessary that at this point in our journey we are moved to seek a deeper understanding and a more loving and practical approach to those who struggle with mental illness in our meetings. There is some truth in the decision of a meeting for clearness to "leave it to the professionals". Most of us are not psychiatrists, psychologists or mental health nurses, but who is to fill the gap between science and spirituality, professional detachment and the warmth of friendship if not ourselves? Yet we do need the benefit of some well-founded, practical advice in addition to not telling somebody who is depressed "to pull themselves together".

I do realise how difficult it is to help people to change their attitudes and the need for courage and wisdom to attempt it, but if we are to be communities of transformation we must attempt it, and be bold as well as cautious:

> "Take heed, dear Friends, to the promptings of love and truth in your hearts. Trust them as the leadings of God whose Light shows us our darkness and brings us to new life."
>
> *Advices & queries* 1

Isobel Lane encourages Friends to put their faith into practice

Mental health in our meetings

Printed in *The Friend*, 24 May 2013

For me, the most vital Quaker testimony is that to equality. If we truly believe that we are created equal, unique, precious, a child of God, how can we treat any human being as not worthy of the same consideration and respect as anyone else? When mental health issues create discomfort (usually due to fear arising from ignorance) living this testimony can become difficult. Experience shows me that ignorance creates fear, and fear is very powerful. The best way that I have found to overcome this is to be as open as I dare in telling others of my realities, so they know why I sometimes behave as I do and, while maybe not liking it, can see that I have not ceased to be human. I also need to feel safe with them. So, it is a slow process. As Bob Johnson says (in his book *Emotional Health*): "Truth and trust are rarely dramatic but you cannot be emotionally fit without them." We have a testimony to truth. If we cannot be truthful among ourselves, how can we follow that testimony in the wider world?

My own story
My own story may illustrate some of the difficulties that meetings have when faced with mental health issues. The last few years have been very difficult for me. I was very ill and spent some months in hospital. Friends from my meeting visited me from time to time to have a meeting for worship with me. That was immensely valuable. After discharge I was still very fragile and fighting a very hard battle within myself. I found that my ministry sometimes disturbed others. I was aware of this and felt alien. The meeting elders responded by producing a leaflet about ministry. This was done sensitively and with truth. I think that helped all of us. I have, also, had to use the meeting to root myself to stop me leaving and harming myself. I found it impossible to speak about this at the time but, later, did so when the power of that feeling had dropped to a manageable level. I was very frightened of revealing my thoughts. I felt they were unacceptable and simply far too much for others to deal or be with. I was also worried that actions that I would find inappropriate might be taken, when what I needed most was human warmth and acceptance of my struggle at the level it was to me.

Lack of awareness

The lack of awareness of the realities of mental illness and, indeed, the fact that it is illness was vividly illustrated in a meeting for healing. At these we speak the names of people who we feel need to be held in the light. My name was not spoken. I was deeply upset. I felt that my illness was considered as not needing healing and how little mental illness is considered, let alone understood. More recently I said that I was struggling badly and did get a response that helped me. A Friend gave me a very warm hug and others spoke to me, including someone who had not previously spoken of her depression, so, in my meeting at least, things are slowly changing. I have heard of at least one case where a Friend in hospital heard nothing at all from his meeting. Why not? If he had a 'physical' illness would he have been neglected? Were the Friends in his meeting afraid? Couldn't they see his need? Or did they simply not care enough? When researching the difficulties that Friends with mental illness have I was told about a situation where a meeting for clearness was held to discern what to do about a Friend with extreme anxiety. Apparently it was decided to 'leave it to the professionals'. I hope that her meeting offered her warmth and simple acceptance as another human being.

Another Friend said that he has difficulty with the idea that people who have mental health problems that make silent worship difficult should consider if a Quaker meeting is the place for them. Surely, the consideration should be the other way round? How can the meeting be more comfortable with that Friend? As another Friend said: "Thinking about this in relation to the testimony to equality, it doesn't seem right to treat these people's needs as any less than the rest of the meeting." Last year a wonderful person, Wanda, from my meeting died. At her Memorial Meeting, a friend of hers said that she had rung Wanda when she was mentally distressed. Wanda had tried to help by offering ideas of things to do about it. The friend found that this simply did not work, so she said to Wanda: "Why can't you just be with me in my pain?" Wanda paused, then simply said: "Thank you." That was a wonderful gift.

Long history of involvement

Quakers have a long history of involvement with mental illness. The Retreat in York was founded in 1796 to be a place where Quakers could recover from mental illness in "an environment that would be both familiar and sympathetic to their needs". Other things have been happening more recently: Young Friends expressed a concern some fifteen years ago and the third London Quaker Dialogue was on the topic of 'Spirituality, Creativity and Mental Illness'. The Friends Fellowship of Healing addressed it in October 2010. The Quaker Youthwork Conference in 2010 held an event on the subject of Young People and Mental Health and Quaker Life held a special interest group at Yearly Meeting Gathering in Canterbury 2011 on mental health in our meetings. This was later followed by a day-long workshop in York. Woodbrooke offers support to elders and overseers through the 'Mental Health in our Meetings' courses. A 'Mental Health Cluster' (MHC), on the Quaker Life Network, has now been formed to carry forward the work within Friends generally. Its members are Stephan Ball, Isobel Lane, Jane Muers and Peter Allen-Williams.

Carrying the work forward

In order to carry the work forward the MHC needs to gather material from Friends with experience of mental health issues in their meetings, from those with mental illness and others, whatever their interest. We aim to show how Friends do, and can – as sufferers, carers, healers and fellow human beings – help all in the meeting to be safe, equal, build trust, be at peace, and, as a consequence, reach deeper levels of awareness and fellowship (Friendship) allowing all to partake fully in the care of the meeting, feel connected and safe and enabling hope to grow. To assist in this we would greatly value anything that you would like to tell us about your own experience, whether positive or not. We plan to find ways of using these personal stories and examples to take our concern further, such as through a special publication or through the new elders and oversight handbook. Everything shared will be treated as confidential. Please tell us whether you wish to be anonymous or not or if you would prefer not to have your contribution used directly. If you are able to contribute something of your own experience, whether as someone with mental illness, a carer, a friend, a Friend within a meeting who has concerns about mental health in the meeting, or as a healer, we would be glad to receive it in confidence care of Oliver Waterhouse at the address below. I would like to finish with a quotation:

"If no one is honest and visible then nobody can move forward at all."

Stephen Amos

Follow-up and resources

To find out more about Quaker involvement in issues related to mental health and distress, including being on an email list, contact Quaker Life Network Mental Health Cluster via Oliver Waterhouse:

oliverw@quaker.org.uk; 020 7663 1007
Quaker Life Network, Quaker Life, Friends House,
173 Euston Road, London NW1 2BJ

For definitions and understanding more about the various diagnoses, mental 'disorders and illnesses' and the help and support available, the following organisations offer clear and easy-to-read leaflets and other resources available online or sometimes in paper form. Helplines have also been included that may be useful. It is also important to be aware of local professional and voluntary resources which will vary from area to area and to make something available in each meeting. Additional advice for Quaker meetings can be found in the Eldership & Oversight Handbook series and in *With a tender hand*, available from the Quaker Centre Bookshop or www.quaker.org.uk/shop.

Mind
www.mind.org.uk
Provide advice and support to empower anyone experiencing a mental health problem. They campaign to improve services, raise awareness and promote understanding. They have a wide range of resources available and information and legal advice lines.

Infoline	0300 123 3393 or text 86463	info@mind.org.uk
Legal advice line	0300 466 6463	legal@mind.org.uk

Lines are open from 9am to 6pm, Monday to Friday (except for bank holidays).

Rethink
www.rethink.org
Provide expert, accredited advice and information to anyone affected by mental health problems. Has over 200 mental health services and 150 support groups across England. Campaigns nationally for policy change, and locally for the support people need.

Helpline	0300 5000 927	info@rethink.org

Lines are open from 10am to 2pm, Monday to Friday.

SANE

www.sane.org.uk

SANE is a UK-wide charity working to improve quality of life for people affected by mental illness. It offers emotional support and information to anyone affected by mental health problems through a helpline, email service and an online Support Forum.

Helpline   0845 767 8000   info@sane.org.uk

Lines are open every evening from 6pm to 11pm.

Mental Health Foundation

www.mentalhealth.org.uk

Research, information, campaigning and advice towards an end to mental ill health and the inequalities that face people experiencing mental distress, living with learning disabilities or reduced mental capacity.

Contact   020 7803 1100

NHS Choices – Your health, your choices

www.nhs.uk

Information from the National Health Service on conditions, treatments, local services and healthy living, with special sections on mental health and dementia.

Mental health information for all

www.rcpsych.ac.uk/healthadvice.aspx

Readable, up-to-date and research-based information and leaflets about mental health problems from the Royal College of Psychiatrists.

Time to Change – Awareness raising

www.time-to-change.org.uk

Focused on raising awareness of mental health issues by using resources to help challenge mental health stigma and discrimination, including tips on how to talk about mental health and information about mental health myths, facts and statistics. A project led by Mind and Rethink Mental Illness.

Dementia

The Alzheimer's Society (England, Wales and Northern Ireland)
www.alzheimers.org.uk
The Alzheimer's Society offers information, advice and support for people with dementia and their families.

    Helpline   0300 222 1122

Lines open from 9am to 5pm, Monday to Friday, and Saturday and Sunday from 10am to 4pm.

Alzheimer Scotland – Action on Dementia
www.alzscot.org
Alzheimer Scotland is the leading dementia organisation in Scotland. They campaign for the rights of people with dementia and their families and provide an extensive range of innovative and personalised support services.

    Helpline   0808 808 3000   helpline@alzscot.org

Open 24 hours

Eating disorders

Beat
www.b-eat.co.uk
Beat is the UK's leading charity supporting anyone affected by eating disorders or difficulties with food, weight and shape.

    Helpline   0845 634 1414   help@b-eat.co.uk
    Youthline   0845 634 7650   fyp@b-eat.co.uk

Lines open from 12pm to 5pm, Monday to Friday (8.30pm Monday and Wednesday).

F.E.A.S.T.
www.feast-ed.org
Families Empowered and Supporting Treatment of Eating Disorders is an international organisation of and for caregivers of people with an eating disorder. F.E.A.S.T. serves families by providing information and mutual support, promoting evidence-based treatment, and advocating for research and education to reduce the suffering associated with eating disorders.

Contact   0330 828 0031   info@feast-ed.org

Acquired Brain Injury

Headway
www.headway.org.uk
Promotes understanding of all aspects of brain injury and provides information, support and services to people with a brain injury, their families and carers. Headway campaigns to reduce incidence of brain injury.

Helpline   0808 800 2244   helpline@headway.org.uk

Lines open from 9am to 5pm, Monday to Friday (answerphone service at other times).